Splitting an Order

TED KOOSER

Splitting an Order

COPPER CANYON PRESS

Port Townsend, Washington

Cover art: Stephen Dinsmore, *Objects on a Grey Table*, 2012. Oil. 30 × 36 × 2 in. Image courtesy of Selby Fleetwood Gallery.

Copper Canyon Press is in residence at Fort Worden State Park in Port Townsend, Washington, under the auspices of Centrum. Centrum is a gathering place for artists and creative thinkers from around the world, students of all ages and backgrounds, and audiences seeking extraordinary cultural enrichment.

LIBRARY OF CONGRESS CATALOGING-IN-PUBLICATION DATA
Kooser, Ted.
[Poems. Selections]
Splitting an order / Ted Kooser.
  pages cm
ISBN 978-1-55659-469-4 (hardback)
I. Title.
PS3561.O6A6   2014
811´.54—dc22

                                                          2014015330

9 8 7 6 5 4 3 2 FIRST PRINTING

Copper Canyon Press
Post Office Box 271
Port Townsend, Washington 98368

www.coppercanyonpress.org

To absent friends

ACKNOWLEDGMENTS

Many of the poems collected here have appeared in the following:
Ames Progressive, The Atlantic, Connecticut Review, Great River Review,
The Hudson Review, Kenyon Review, The Laurel Review, Margie,
Mid-American Review, The Midwest Quarterly, Midwestern Miscellany,
Moon City Review, Narrative, The Nebraska Poets' Calendar, New Century
North American Poets, Nimrod, Northwest Florida Review, Ploughshares,
Poetry, Potomac Review, Prairie Schooner, River Styx, River Teeth, Solo,
South Dakota Review, Virginia Quarterly Review, and *Willow Review.*

"Estate Sale" was originally published in 1995 in a limited, thirty-copy
edition entitled *A Book of Things,* by Joseph Ruffo under his imprint,
Lyra Press, Lincoln, Nebraska.

"Splitting an Order" first appeared in *Out of That Moment,* Brooding Heron
Press, Waldron, Washington, 2006.

"Small Rooms in Time" was first published in *River Teeth* and then in
The Best American Essays 2005 (edited by Susan Orlean).

A number of these poems were included in *Together,* a limited letterpress
edition published in 2012 by Brooding Heron Press.

My thanks to my wife, Kathleen Rutledge, and to David Baker, Marsha
Cooper, James Crews, Dan Gerber, Judith Harris, Jim Harrison, Bob King,
and Connie Wanek, all of whom have offered helpful suggestions for many
of these poems. And to the memory of my dear friend and mentor, Leonard
Nathan, whose guidance is ever with me.

As the Lord liveth, and as thy soul liveth,
I will not leave thee. And they two went on.

2 KINGS 2:6

Contents

I

~~~

II

~~~

III

~~~

Splitting an Order

I

Two Men on an Errand

The younger, a balloon of a man
in his sixties with some of the life
let out of him, sags on the cheap couch
in the car repair shop's waiting room.
Scuffed shoes, white socks, blue trousers,
a nondescript gray winter jacket.
His face is pale, and his balding head
nods with some kind of palsy. His fists
stand like stones on the tops of his thighs—
white boulders, alabaster—and the flesh
sinks under the weight of everything
those hands have squeezed. The other man
is maybe eighty-five, thin and bent
over his center. One foot swollen
into a foam-rubber sandal, the other
tight in a hard black shoe. Blue jeans,
black jacket with a semi tractor
appliquéd on the back, white hair
fine as a cirrus cloud. He leans
forward onto a cane, with both hands
at rest on its handle as if it were
a steering wheel. The two sit hip to hip,
a bony hip against a fleshy one,
talking of car repairs, about the engine
not hitting on all the cylinders.
It seems the big man drove them here,
bringing the old man's car, and now
they are waiting, now they have to wait
or want to wait until the next thing

happens, and they can go at it
together, the younger man nodding,
the older steering with his cane.

110th Birthday

Helen Stetter

Born into an age of horse-drawn wagons
that knocked and rocked over rutted mud
in the hot wake of straw, manure and flies,
today she glides to her birthday party
in a chair with sparkling carriage wheels,
along a lane of smooth gray carpeting
that doesn't jar one petal of the pink corsage
pinned to her breast. Her hair is white
and light as milkweed down, and her chin
thrusts forward into the steady breezes
out of the next year, and the next and next.
Her eyelids, thin as old lace curtains,
are drawn over dreams, and her fingers
move only a little, touching what happens
next, no more than a breath away. Her feet,
in fuchsia bedroom slippers, ride inches above
the world's hard surface, up where she belongs,
safe from the news, and now and then, as if
with secret pleasure, she bunches her toes
the way a girl would, barefoot in sand
along the Niobrara, just a century ago.

Near a Mall

On a hot, windy day, at the hour
when people get off work, I saw
along a busy street an Asian man
with long black hair, carrying
a rubber chicken-suit, his arms
clasped round its waist. The chicken,
a good foot taller, half of its air
let out, was alive in the breeze,
its wild-eyed head with red comb
and slack beak bobbing and pecking,
though it was losing, its soft claws
knuckles-down over the concrete.
Passersby were honking and laughing,
giving a thumbs-up, a high-sign
to the little man, his long hair
tossed across his sweaty face,
wrestling his chicken, his place of
employment, within which all day
he'd been making a living,
peering out through a slit
and waving his wings as we passed.

Splitting an Order

I like to watch an old man cutting a sandwich in half,
maybe an ordinary cold roast beef on whole wheat bread,
no pickles or onion, keeping his shaky hands steady
by placing his forearms firm on the edge of the table
and using both hands, the left to hold the sandwich in place,
and the right to cut it surely, corner to corner,
observing his progress through glasses that moments before
he wiped with his napkin, and then to see him lift half
onto the extra plate that he asked the server to bring,
and then to wait, offering the plate to his wife
while she slowly unrolls her napkin and places her spoon,
her knife, and her fork in their proper places,
then smooths the starched white napkin over her knees
and meets his eyes and holds out both old hands to him.

An Incident

On the sidewalk in front of the parking garage, a blind man who has fallen is attended by three firemen, a medic, and two policemen, all of whom squat on their heels and by so doing cover the fallen man with shadow. He sits among them with his legs splayed out, undoubtedly feeling their shadows putting cool hands on his face, and he reaches out a long way through darkness to rest his white fingers on the shoulder of his seeing-eye dog, a big, dull-looking black retriever, whose tongue is dripping, for this is a warm day in October, the afternoon sun tiny but fierce in the sky. The dog's plain face is bright with uneasy patience and the blind man's eyes are wide and white, as if a hand had risen up from the darkness inside him and taken his heart in its grip and pulled him down.

Two fire trucks and a squad car idle in the street. People are stopping nearby to see what has happened and what will happen next. Each of us is filled to the throat with some part of the same one fear, as if we had been gathered here to bear it away, and now a few of us turn from the fallen man and walk away or get back into our cars, each of us carrying part of the man's great fear, and it seems that perhaps because of this he now is feeling better, as he gets to his feet in the opening circle and shakes out his arms as if he were suddenly lighter.

Bad News

Because it arrives while you sleep,
it's the one call you never pick up
on the first ring. In that pause between
the fourth and what would be the fifth,
in the flare of a lamp you've snapped on,
there it is, having waited all night
until it was time to awaken you,
shaping its sentence over and over,
simple old words you lean into
as into a breath from a cave.
And once the news is out, thrown over
your shoulders like a threadbare robe,
you move on cold feet room to room,
feeling as weightless as a soul,
turning on every light in the house,
needing the light all around you
because it's a new day now, though still
in darkness, hours before dawn,
a day you'll learn to call *that* day,
the first morning after it happened.

Swinging from Parents

The child walks between her father and mother,
holding their hands. She makes the shape of the *y*
at the end of *infancy,* and lifts her feet
the way the *y* pulls up its feet, and swings
like the *v* in *love,* between an *o* and an *e*
who are strong and steady and as far as she knows
will be there to swing from forever. Sometimes
her father, using his free hand, points to something
and says its name, the way the arm of the *r*
points into the future at the end of *father.*
Or the *r* at the end of *forever.* It's that *forever*
the child puts her trust in, lifting her knees,
swinging her feet out over the world.

Potatoes

On a misty, sepia-and-green
May morning, crossing Iowa,
I saw from the highway
a man, a woman, and a horse
out sowing seed potatoes,
using a two-wheeled planter
from a hundred years ago,
the man beneath a straw hat,
holding the horse's reins
and taking a sight on the posts
at the end of the field,
the woman perched behind,
above the tin potato bin,
watching the steel disc roll along
and fold the earth back under.
The horse was brown as varnish
as it pulled us forward, all
of us, with black clay dropping
from its shoes, and I was
never surer of the world.

At Arby's, at Noon

Some of us were arriving, hungry,
impatient, while others had eaten
and were leaving, bidding goodbye
to our friends, and among us
stood a pretty young woman, blind,
her perfect fingers interwoven
about the top of her cane,
and she was bending forward,
open eyed, to find the knotted lips
of a man whose disfigured face
had been assembled out of scars
and who was leaving, hurrying off,
and though their kiss was brief
and askew and awkwardly pursed,
we all received it with a kind of
wonder, and kept it on our lips
through the afternoon.

A Meeting after Many Years

Our words were a few colorful leaves
afloat on a very old silence,
the kind with a terrifying undertow,
and we stood right at its edge,
wrapping ourselves in our own arms
because of the chill, and with old voices
called back and forth across all those years
until we could bear it no longer,
and turned from each other,
and walked away into our countries.

The Rollerblader

I saw her coming from a long way off,
that singular, side-to-side, whisk-broom movement
as she swung her arms and legs, brushing
the morning and its inertia aside,
and the dew which throughout the cool night
had settled on the path like starlight.
An old man and woman, too, with their little dog,
were swept off into the grass, lifting their knees,
and they glanced at her hot red face as she passed,
as if they'd known her once, and all that fury.

In a Gift Shop

Only in recent years have I begun
to notice them living among us,
and yesterday there were two more,
the one somewhere in her seventies
and in a wheelchair, and the other
younger by maybe twenty years,
helping the older woman pick out cards
from one of those squeaky revolving
racks in a shop. The older would gesture
with a weak brush of her hand to tell
the younger to turn the rack a little
and the younger would turn it, and both
would study the cards from the top
to the bottom, and once in a while
the younger would take a card down
and show it to the other, holding it
closed and then open, and the older
might nod to agree that it seemed
the right choice, or she might dismiss it
with a shake of her head with its thin
white hair, and the younger would
patiently put it back, and this went on
for what seemed a very long while
as the woman in the wheelchair slowly
assembled a little collection of cards
in her lap, and the rack turned round
as if it were the world itself (though with
a plaintive squeak), with the colorful days
passing first into the light and then out

and with hundreds of thousands of women
like these, each helping another
do something for someone not there.

Changing Drivers

Their nondescript, late-model car
is pulled off on the windy shoulder,
its doors flung wide, and the driver
gets out, gripping the roof with a hand
and lifting himself just as the woman
gets out of her side, both of them stiff,
both kneading the small of their backs,
rolling their heads on their necks,
squinting into the midday sun.
Then the driver starts out around
the front bumper, swinging his legs
as if they weren't his, his thin hair lifting,
just as the woman straightens herself
and sets out around the trunk, holding
her permanent's white curls in place
with both hands, both man and woman
calling a few words back and forth
across the axis of the car's hot roof
as they stoop and fit themselves inside
and the car's springs settle a little,
and each of them reaches a long way out
to pull the doors shut, her door first
then his, and they rock and shift,
fastening their belts, then both of them
lean forward, almost simultaneously,
and peer into their side-view mirrors
to see whatever is bearing down
from wherever they've been, and together
they ease out over the crunching gravel
onto the highway and move on.

Snapshot

Light's hand is swift, its penmanship
neat and precise. It jotted down a memo
on this square of paper, then left it behind,
a lost list of shadows burned by a paper clip
rusting away. Five men in half-light,
standing under the roof of an open porch,
holding a string of dead mallards.
One man grins and points at the camera,
his fingertip bright as a spark, reaching out,
touching the shimmering film of the future.

Two

On a parking lot staircase
I met two fine-looking men
descending, both in slacks
and dress shirts, neckties
much alike, one of the men
in his sixties, the other
a good twenty years older,
unsteady on his polished shoes,
a son and his father, I knew
from their looks, the son with his
right hand on the handrail,
the father, left hand on the left,
and in the middle they were
holding hands, and when I neared,
they opened the simple gate
of their interwoven fingers
to let me pass, then reached out
for each other and continued on.

While We Were Passing

As if it were waiting for someone,
the house faced the road, its door
held open by a little bronze dog,
the lace curtains at its windows
drawn back and tied, so the parlor
must have been warm and yellow
with a welcoming light.

The siding had been freshly painted
a sticky-looking white, with green
screened windows and the customary
battleship-gray on the floor of the porch,
where two plain kitchen chairs
were turned to face each other
as if prepared for conversation.

The grass was recently mowed,
and clipped by hand around the stones
that lined the footpath to the door,
and the clippings had been swept away.
This happened the last Sunday in May,
and on either side of the porch
were peonies droopy with blossoms.

And it looked as if someone had recently
picked up the petals that had fallen,
though more were falling as we passed,
petal by petal, in the indifferent,
casual manner of peonies, and perhaps
someone was standing just inside
and watching them fall, almost

feeling them fall, and was waiting
to come out again now that we
had passed, to pick up more of them,
one hand packing them like tissues
into the other, keeping an eye on the place
where the road came toward her
wide and empty out of the trees.

Gabardine

To sit in sunlight with other old men,
none with his legs crossed, our feet in loose shoes
hot and flat on the earth, hands curled in our laps
or on our knees, like birds that now and then
fly up with our words and then settle again
in a slightly different way, casting a slightly
different shadow over our pant legs, gabardine,
blue, gray or brown, warmed by the passing sun.

The Woman Whose Husband Was Dying

She turned her eyes from mine, for within mine
she knew there wasn't room for all her sorrow.
She needed a plain that she could flood with grief,
and as she stood there by the door I saw the distance
before her slowly filling, as if from hidden springs,
and she stepped outside, and placed one foot
and then the other on the future, and it held her up.

II

Estate Sale

At a broken window, an old cobweb
wadded and rolled by the wind:
one of those long woolen stockings
your grandmother wore.

~~~

The parts of a broken birdfeeder,
put into a box for fixing later,
the lid warped on its hinges,
its tiny white feathers of paint
loose to the touch, one of the side boards
split—but the pieces saved, the board
where the birds sat down to eat
now rotted and black from the rains.
In the slot where the glass once fit,
a few seeds missed by the mice,
some of them sprouted but dead now,
the pale wings stiffly folded.

~~~

An empty coffee can
wrapped in aluminum foil.
In this poor urn, the peonies
rode to the graveyard,
covering their faces
with immaculate gloves.

~~~

A baseball with one of its seams
split wide, its skin
mottled and green, a planet
with one of its mountain ranges
blown open, displaying
a kind of universe, electrons
spinning, leaving their vapor trails.

~~~

The nest of some tiny bird,
each blade of dead grass
spun into its place
on the potter's wheel
of her busy movements,
preparing a vessel for song.

~~~

A soggy shoe box, and in its grayness
a yellow tin of corn pads rising
sun-like over the reflecting pools
of a neatly folded pair of glasses.

~~~

In its tattered paper sleeve,
a 78-rpm record, Blue Label
with dog and Victrola,
dust sealing the grooves.
If we had the means to play it,
over the music we'd hear
the rhythmical cough

of a woman who once
bent toward the turning disc
and tried to sing along.

~~~

Clipped into a sleeve of waxed paper,
a lock of hair tied with a ribbon
the color of water, the hair too yellow
to have been real, but perhaps, when
left to itself like the colors in memories,
grown brighter with time.

~~~

A windup wristwatch
with a cracked leather band:
throughout his life, a man
may out of curiosity
push his hand up to the wrist
through a hole in the fence
of time, and then, one day
as he leans there enjoying
the hours, someone comes up
on the other side, takes hold,
and pulls him through.

~~~

The red, webbed collar for a dog,
bristled and frayed to a foamy white
where it bit back hard at the buckle.

~~~

A section of unused stovepipe
standing unsnapped and open
like somebody's coat, and in it
the thin blue smoke of a spiderweb.

~~~

Five or six feet of heavy black
electrical wire gathered up into
a few loose coils like a lariat,
the last few inches of each end
brought over and under the coils
and then very carefully twisted
into a tight little pigtail,
the tarry insulation drawing back
from neat, clean cuts that let
the inner wires—white, black,
and the bright green ground—
push out of the darkness
like the first shoots of a lily,
smooth tubes through which
the tips of copper petals ease.

~~~

A 25-amp glass fuse.
Under the clear ice of its surface
it is easy to see the silver ribbon
of a motionless fish,
its body aligned with the current.

~~~

An envelope of dime-store
photo mounting corners—
little black bats that seem always
to wait at the edges.

~~~

A bucket of white, coiled springs
from a rotten hammock,
each with the tight muscularity
of a living thing, drawn back
against itself, defensive,
every nerve tuned to a snarl.

~~~

A wooden cheese box with a blue horse
impressed in the side—big mare
in blinders, head lowered and pulling hard
at a wagon of cream cans. A man
in a hat with his face in blue shadow
up on the seat, reins loose in his hands.
The cheese box is easing its seams
under the load of a dozen burned-out
spark plugs, its thin brads loose
in their rusty holes, the side slats
split, the dead plugs tumbled together,
muscle to muscle, dark smears of oil
on their tight white letter-sweaters.

~~~

On a nail, a chain fish-stringer
with a few scales stuck to its open hooks.
Give it a shake and it whips and glitters
in muscular waves,
throwing off light like drops of water.

~~~

What can be read in the open book
of an old brass door hinge? Here are two
in a coffee can, one of them coated
with cream-colored paint and one brown,
the first from a door that once swung
into the kitchen and out, fanning
the fragrance of pot roast, its paint
worried and chipped; the other from
the cold brown door to the attic stairs
that was rarely opened, behind which stood
winter, wearing an old woolen coat
with mothballs loose in his pockets.
The first hinge swung smooth on a film
of black oil from bacon and chops;
the other cried out through the frost.

~~~

The wooden wheel in this old pulley
had nowhere to roll away to,
so it stayed right here in its iron harness,
whining and whining.

~~~

A folded wooden clotheshorse,
its creamy ribs like bone,
like a beach umbrella blown inside out
by the cold sea-wind of time,
and next to this, a galvanized tub
in which a washboard leans
like a staircase up into the present.

~~~

In a tin can, a packet of spinach seeds
folded over and paper-clipped,
with a neat hole chewed in the side
and the seeds all eaten but one:
a tiny brown leather valise
packed with green scarves.

~~~

A tire that was never used,
still wrapped in paper swaddling—
old road maps, maybe, soaked
and smoothed around it like poultices
to cool the lust for rolling.

~~~

A discarded billfold, its breathing
shallow, a clam with a brown hinge
polished by wear, the halves
closed loosely over the flattened pearl
of a buffalo nickel.

~~~

And among these homely things,
an antique gilded harp,
its dusty strings like a curtain
drawn over the silence,
stroked by fingers of light.

Opossum

You were not at all startled to see me
when I snapped on a light in the barn
and caught you with your curled tail
clutching a bundle of pin oak leaves
you'd been out collecting for your nest
under the floor. In a brain no bigger
than a pumpkin seed, there's not much room
for fear, and none for self-admiration,
so I have pushed aside some of my own fear
to admire you. You have soft fur
like milkweed down, and bright black eyes
alive with all the big and little things
you've learned from midnight, using
your soft pink nose and your restless
pink fingers. It is those fingers that might
make a person fear you, for they seem
almost human, greedy and dangerous.
I think you may know this, because you
slowly turned toward me and lifted
one of your hands to show me how it could
grasp and squeeze a tiny piece of the light
that fell between us, and even a piece
of my breath.

A Backyard Fish Pool

In autumn, a flimsy coverlet
lay over its surface, pieced
from brown and yellow leaves,
a pretty thing, under a glaze
of rain, and a boy could pull it
apart with a stick and peer down
into a black like none other,
cold and solemn as the past,
a lens atop the other autumns
that had come and gone and now
lay sunken, woven of leaves
that still showed just a little
of their color, layered years
that knew all that had happened
but were silent, that when I
stirred them with my stick
became a swirling cloud
that surfaced with a mortal smell.

A Visitant at Five A.M.

It was there on the arm of my rocker
when I turned on the floor lamp,
a tiny moth clipped from the edge
of the night before, gray upon gray
like a dirty city, wings coated with odors
and noise, the beep of a backing truck,
the smells from a seafood restaurant,
waxy sweetness of lipstick. And as soon
as the light grew strong enough to lift it
it was gone, smoke to the shadows,
taking with it the fur collar that brushed
my cheek, a wisp of hair across my lips,
the request that the band never played,
and it was morning, and the house was cold.

A Jonathan in Spring

For Maxine Kumin

An apple tree may live about as long
as a horse, and our old Jonathan,
now rickety and lame with foot rot,
must surely be close to its end, but today
it leans into yet another March,
wheezing with bees. Each spring we think
we've seen the last of its cedar-spotted,
tart abundance, then September arrives
and there in the dew and leafy grass
lie those familiar, rusty harness bells,
and as they drop around us we can hear
the sound of galloping.

Dead Bat

When I slid out my heavy thrift-store
hide-a-bed to sweep around it, then
shoved it back, it left behind a bat
that must have been shaken out of
one of the springs where I imagine
it hung for years like a burned-out bulb.
It was frail and almost weightless,
as if a boy (the very boy I'd been)
had glued it together out of balsa sticks
and scraps of papery skin, and I held it up
eye-level as you would a paper plane
and flew it about. Its nasty face with its
needle teeth was turned up, ready
to snatch whatever it saw out there
banking and darting and weaving
ahead in the gloomy afterlife, and after
I'd dropped it with a little rustle
into my big black plastic bag of trash,
I went back twice to see if it had moved.

Sundial

Two friends, dead now for many years,
bought it for us one Christmas,
picked it out of a Crate & Barrel catalog
and had it shipped with a little card
with love in someone else's hand,
a perfunctory gift, as ours to them
must surely have been, perhaps a local
cheese, a few small jars of jam or jelly,
not gift so much as habit, like a handshake,
touch and go, and for years it has lain
on the earth in our garden, telling time
to no one but the fallen curls of leaves
from the ornamental crab, its gnomon
a cattail standing in a pond of bronze,
swinging its shadow past a little turtle,
also cast in bronze, forever wading
into the next hour, followed by the rest.

Birdhouse

The rusty screw-eye had worked its way
out of the roof, and the house had dropped
through a shaft in the early summer air
like an elevator. It had struck the earth
and toppled, and had lain there days
before I picked it up—a sodden weight—
and pried it open, dug out the moldy nest
of twigs and bits of leaves and feathers,
and found three tiny, shattered eggs,
sticky with strings of yoke, and among them
dozens of ants that I'd disturbed, each with
an egg of her own, white as a grain of rice,
and no place, now, to set it down.

Tree Frog

It's the watery grays and greens
of the silver maple from which
it descended, ambling leg over leg
through an all-night summer rain,
this dollop of life now sound asleep
on the porch steps, in the first gray
light of dawn, just one step up
from the puddled walk, as if
in the cold black early hours
it had started the arduous climb
toward home but had only the strength
for a start. Touched by my finger,
it moves only a little, hunching up,
not ready for another day,
its legs pulled in, its job so deeply
tucked away that it might never again
lean trilling on an evening's doorbell.
But look, one eye is open now,
or partly open, and the day starts here,
below the dripping, tallest-ever tree,
starts here for all of us.

Lantern

In the predawn cold and darkness,
it was only a pinch of light,
not more than a cup of warmth,
as a farmer carried it over the snow
to the barn where his dozen cows
stood stomping, heavy with milk
in the milky cloud of their lowing.
But that was many years ago,
and his lantern has rusted,
its last fumes lost on the seasons
like the breath of those cows.
But at the last he thought to leave
a fresh ribbon of wick coiled up
in the chimney in case it was ever
needed again, a dollar's worth
of preparation. And, getting prepared
for a later winter, a pregnant mouse
was able to squeeze through a vent
and unravel that wick and make
a cottony nest with dusty,
panoramic windows, and there to raise
her bald and mewling, pissy brood,
and then for them to disappear,
the way we all, one day, move on,
leaving a little sharp whiff
of ourselves in the dirty bedding.

Dead Fly

This black sedan lies on its top
on the kitchen windowsill, its wheels
in the air, its battery drained,
the oil trickling into the cylinders.
It must have happened during the night
when no one was around to see,
and it looks as if someone has been here
early this morning to pop the trunk
and crawl in under it to take out
something. But I am only barely
curious, continuing on as I am,
doing my few breakfast dishes,
fussy to get all the egg from the tines
of my fork, and then from the spatula
and the weary old skillet that has seen
so much, and me with the morning
picking up speed, the days streaming past,
hot suds backfiring on my hands.

Garrison, Nebraska

The north-south streets are named for poets—
Longfellow, Whittier, Bryant, Lowell—
so it's no surprise that this tiny village
is fading to gray, mildewed and dusty,
shelved at the back of the busy library
of American progress. On this winter day
all that is left of Whittier's "Snow-Bound"
whispers in under the nailed-shut door
of a house at the edge of a cornfield,
and slides across a red vinyl car seat
wedged in a broken tree. All but a few
stubborn families have packed up and left,
seeking a better life, following Evangeline,
leaving this island with its cars up on blocks,
its gardens of broken washing machines,
its empty rabbit hutches nailed to sheds,
cold and alone on the sea of the prairie,
to be pounded and pounded forever
by time and these whitecaps of snow.

A Mouse in a Trap

A tiny wood raft was afloat
on the cold gray sea
of the cellar floor, and to it
a dead mouse clung,
trailing its legs and tail, the ship
of the rest of its life
swallowed up without leaving
so much as a ripple.
I felt the firm deck of the day
tilt just a little, as if all of us
living, surviving, had rushed
to one side to look down.

A Wasp's Nest

All day she's busy in the bell
that hangs by our door, an antique
from a sea-buoy, cast in brass.
We rarely ring it, living alone
with no one to call from the fields,
so it's fine that she's chosen
to build at the heart of that silence.

All day she flies from somewhere,
up into the darkness and away,
abdomen glistening, heavy with eggs,
black legs trailing out like streamers.
As she fashions her palace,
tower by tower, all paper and paste,
her hot whine teases a note
from the bell, clear and haunting,
guiding us on through the narrows
and into the generations.

Tree Removal

First the boom truck offers its cup
to the sixty-foot elm, just a sip
from a cheap white plastic mug
after all those years of service
fishing for weather. Then follows
wave upon wave of the chainsaw,
a hot spray of sawdust.
But the tree makes its exit with grace,
going down slowly, one piece at a time,
hauling in the cool net of its shadow
and patiently folding it
into the boat of the clouds.

Barn Swallows

Here are all of the days in August
marked off in sharp strokes
on the power wire out to the barn.
Each year at this time they line up
for roll call, parents and young,
leaving their mud cups empty
under the eaves, on beams and rafters,
on the lintels of doors. In dark blue
iridescent ink they write
their thank-you note: Where once
we were few we now are many!
And the next day they're gone,
wiped from the sky by a rag of cloud
just as the first leaf falls.

Zinc Lid

It's the gray of canning-season rain,
neither cool nor warm, and mottled
with feeble light. There's a moony
milk-glass insert ringed by rubber
and a dent where somebody rapped it
to break the seal. But its cucumber
summers, dill and brine, are over.
No more green mason jars cooling,
no generations of dust beneath
the cellar stairs, the ancient quarts
of tomatoes like balls of wax,
the pickles slowly going gray
as kidneys, pale applesauce settling
out of its syrup. Today, on a bench
in a dark garage it's upside down,
a miniature galvanized tub adrift
on time, and in it two survivors,
a bolt that once held everything
together, season in and season out,
and a wing nut resting its wings.

III

At a Kitchen Table

Not a flock of stories,
not usually,
but a few that arrive at dusk,
in pairs, quietly
creating themselves
in the feathery light.
And rarely with fancy plumage
of blue or green or red
but plain, as of clay or wood,
with a plain little song.
Theirs are the open wings
we light our table by.

A Morning in Early Spring

First light, and under stars
our elm glides out of darkness
to settle on its nest of shadows,
spreading its feathers to shake out

the night. Above, a satellite—
one shining bead of mercury
bearing thousands of voices—
rolls toward the light in the east.

The Big Dipper, for months left
afloat in a bucket of stars,
has begun to leak. Each morning
it settles a little into the north.

A rabbit bounces over the yard
like a knot at the end of a rope
that the new day reels in, tugging
the night and coiling it away.

A fat robin bobs her head,
hemming a cloth for her table,
pulling the thread of a worm,
then neatly biting it off.

My wife, in an old velour robe,
steps off a fifty-yard length
of the dawn, out to the road
to get the newspaper, each step

with its own singular sound.
Each needle in the windbreak
bends to the breeze, the windmill
turns clockwise then ticks to a stop.

No other day like this one.
A crocus like a wooden match—
Ohio Blue Tip—flares in the shadows
that drip from the downspout.

This is a morning that falls between
weathers, a morning that hangs
dirty gray from the sky,
like a sheet from a bachelor's bed,

hung out to dry but not dry yet,
the air not warm or cool,
and my wife within it, bearing the news
in both hands, like a tray.

Along the road to east and west,
on the dark north side of fence posts,
thin fingers of shadowy snowdrifts
pluck and straighten the fringe

on a carpet of fields. Clouds float in
like ships flying the pennants of geese,
and the trees, like tuning forks,
begin to hum. Now a light rain

fingers the porch roof, trying
the same cold key over and over.
Spatters of raindrops cold as dimes,
and a torn gray curtain of cloud

floats out of a broken window
of sky. Icy patches of shadows
race over the hills. No other day
like this one, not ever again.

Now, for only a moment, sleet
sifts across the shingles, pale beads
threaded on filaments of rain,
and the wind dies. A threadbare

pillowcase of snow is shaken out
then draped across the morning,
too thin to cover anything for long.
None other like this.

All winter, the earth was sealed
by a lid of frost, like the layer
of paraffin over the apple jelly,
or the white disk of chicken fat

on soup left to cool, but now,
in cold tin sheds with dripping roofs,
old tractors warm their engines,
burning the feathery mouse nests

from red exhausts, rattling the jars
of cotter pins, shaking gaskets
on nails and stirring the dirty rags
of cobwebs. And young farmers

who have already this morning
put on the faces of ancestors
and have shoved the cold red fists
of grandfathers, fathers, and uncles

deep in their pockets, stand framed
in wreaths of diesel smoke,
looking out over the wet black fields
from doors that open into spring.

In first light I bend to one knee.
I fill the old bowl of my hands
with wet leaves, and lift them
to my face, a rich broth of browns

and yellows, and breathe the vapor,
spiced with oils and, I suspect,
just a pinch of cumin. This is my life,
none other like this.

Closing the Windows

First, the uncertain white fingers
of lightning, fumbling around
with the black hem of the county,
peering in under, then thunder,
then the flat slap of the first drop
on the roof, like a fingertip
tapping, "Right here, put the rain
here." And then my father
in his summer pajamas
moving in silhouette, closing
the windows, no word from him
who swept through the house
like a flashing shadow, but a chatter
of leaves blown over the shingles,
the clunk of sash weights
deep in the walls, then the storm
muffled by spattered glass.
It was all so ordinary then
to see him at the foot of the bed,
closing a squeaky window,
but more than sixty years have passed
and now I understand that it was
not so ordinary after all.

The Past

What we remember of it
is what we began to memorize
as children, rehearsing
the same scenes again and again
until we got them perfect,
the father, the mother, the sister
entering from left and right,
obeying the arrows and Xs
chalked onto the stage,
saying their lines precisely
as we would have them said
until these dramas were fixed
in tableaux, enameled mannequins
nodding in storefronts,
raising their hands to comfort
or strike, while our shapes
in the shimmering glass
appear to be standing among them.
And if someone should call
one of our scenes into question,
we rush to its defense,
afraid that the window will crack
and collapse with a crash
and we will have nowhere to turn
to see ourselves reflected
in what we have so carefully
created and directed.

Sleep Apnea

Night after night, when I was a child,
I woke to the guttering candle
of my father's breath. It made a sound
like the starlings that sometimes
got caught in our chimney, a chirping
that would gradually, steadily build
to a desperate, flat slapping of wings,
then suddenly drop into silence,
into the thick soot at the bottom
of midnight. No silence was ever
so deep. And then, after maybe
a minute or two, I would hear
a twitter as he came to life again,
and could at last take a breath for myself,
a sip like a toast, lifting a chilled glass
of air, wishing us courage, those of us
lying awake through those hours,
my mother, my sister and I, who each night
listened to death kiss the fluttering lips
of my father, who slept through it all.

First Marriage

Neither of us would clean the aquarium,
a green box under our troubled roof,
stuffed with mementos nobody wanted.
Sometimes it fluttered with a silvery light,
the only sign of life for months on end.
Nor would either of us feed the fish,
but made them eat what they found
in that murky, weedy silence. At the end
of the marriage, when we divided our things,
we gave the aquarium away, and the woman
who came for it dipped into the green,
and from a couple of dozen fish we'd had
there were only two left, large Silver Dollars
that had thrived on neglect, and eaten the others,
and grown as big as the palms of our hands,
which hung, not touching, guilty at our sides.

Grandfather

A breeze chased his pipe smoke
out over the river, and later he followed,
carrying all of his tackle.

Howard

Our old white lab lies on the stoop,
watching the predawn darkness
stealing from tree to tree beyond him,
a slight disturbance in the light
like a flaw in a pane of glass,
and wary, too, this shape that keeps
its eyes on Howard, bright as a moon
under the porch light. And I'd guess
it probably knows that he can
smell it too, its rippling scent a cold
that floats on the rest of the cold
like a snake on a pool, and maybe
it thinks that this old sphinx
with his stiffening joints might still
be able, suddenly, to come to life
and chase and catch and kill
whatever he has a hunger for,
though he and I know different.

Deep Winter

In the cold blue shadow behind a shed,
among young ash and mulberry trees
standing in discarded tires, and next to
a roll of used and reused sheep wire
and a sheaf of rusty posts, I am alone
among the others who have stood here
as they looked out over the snowy fields,
holding their breath against the stillness,
against our awareness of each other,
whole generations empty between us
like gaps between saplings, all of us
having come tracking through winter
to look for something to use to prop
up something else, or for a part
of a part, and not having found it,
standing both inside and outside of time,
becoming a piece of some great, rusty work
we seem to fit exactly.

New Moon

How much it must bear on its back,
a great ball of blue shadow,
yet somehow it shines, keeps up
an appearance. For hours tonight,
I walked beneath it, learning.
I want to be better at carrying sorrow.
If my face is a mask, formed over
the shadows that fill me,
may I smile on the world like the moon.

Hands in the Wind

Today I drove through a cloud of leaves,
pale oak leaves the color of hands
blown over the street, straight toward me
out of the empty parking lot
of the abandoned Kmart, their fingers
swirling about me, feeling all over my car,
over it, under it. I don't very often
go past there; they must have been waiting
a very long time to have been so
excited to see me. They had probably
blown there from trees in the cemetery
just down the block and had gathered
to wait, folded over each other,
faded old hands with brown liver spots,
young hands with a sheen to their skin.
Then, when they'd seen my car coming,
they'd rushed out into the traffic. It felt
as if all of the people I've loved
were suddenly swirling about me,
wanting to touch me, wishing me well.
I found myself laughing. It all
happened so quickly, and then they were
gone. In the rearview mirror
there were only a few leaves still flying,
a few fluttering down. They had settled
in drifts by the curb, interlacing their fingers.
They'd made a mistake. It hadn't been I
whom they'd meant to make happy.
They'd thought I was somebody else.

Spanish Lessons

My wife moves from room to room,
touching our humble belongings
with a wand of new words—
the iron, the coffeepot, the radio—
making them notice themselves
for the first time in years.
In the kitchen, I hear her
cracking a few round syllables
into a pan of *agua*, followed soon
by a brisk, guttural bubbling,
and later she's climbing the stairs
with an armload of colorful noises,
dropping a few shaggy petals
on every other step. She's going
to fill the bathtub now and scatter
fresh flowers of language
over the surface, then lie there
steeping among them, calling out
the new names for shampoo,
for bath mat, toilet and toothbrush,
lying there with her ears just out of
the water, loving the echoes.

Painting the Barn

The ghost of my good dog, Alice,
sits at the foot of my ladder,
looking up, now and then touching
the bottom rung with her paw.
Even a spirit dog can't climb
an extension ladder, and so,
with my scraper, bucket, and brush,
I am up here alone, hanging on
with one hand in the autumn wind,
high over the earth that Alice
knew so well, every last inch,
and there she sits, whimpering
in just the way the chilly wind
whines under the tin of the roof—
sweet Alice, dear Alice, good Alice,
waiting for me to come down.

Those Summer Evenings

My father would, with a little squeak
and a shudder in the water pipes,
turn on the garden hose, and sprinkle
the honeysuckle bushes clipped
to window height, so that later,
as we slept atop our rumpled sheets
with windows open to the scritch
of crickets, whatever breeze
might flirt its way between
our house and the neighbors'
would brush across the honeysuckle,
sweet and wet, and keep us cool.

Awakening

How heavy it is, this bucket
drawn out of the lake of sleep
with a dream spilling over,
so heavy that on some mornings
you can't quite pull it free
so let it slip back under,
back into the darkness where
the water is warm, even warmer,
but the dream, like a minnow,
has swum away and is merely
a flash in the murky distance,
and the weight of waking up
seems even heavier. But somehow
you lift it again, its handle
biting into your fingers,
and haul it out and set it down
still rippling, a weighty thing
like life itself, in which you dip
the leaky cup of your hands
and drink.

A Person of Limited Palette

I would love to have lived out my years
in a cottage a few blocks from the sea,
and to have spent my mornings painting
out in the cold, wet rocks, to be known
as "a local artist," a pleasant old man
who "paints passably well, in a traditional
manner," a person of limited palette:
earth tones and predictable blues, cloth cap
and cardigan, baggy old trousers
and comfortable shoes, but none of this
shall come to pass, for every day
the possibilities grow fewer, like swallows
in autumn. If you should come looking
for me, you'll find me here, in Nebraska,
thirty miles south of the broad Platte River,
under the flyway of dreams.

IV

Small Rooms in Time

A few years ago, a fifteen-year-old boy answered the side door of a house where I once lived, and was murdered, shot twice by one of five people—two women and three men—who had gone there to steal a pound of cocaine. The boy died just inside the door, at the top of a staircase that led to the cellar where I once had set up my easel and painted. The robbers—all but one still in their teens—stepped over the body, rushed down the steps, and shot three people there, a woman and two men.

Somebody called the police, perhaps the people who rented the apartment on the second floor. The next day's front-page story reported that the three in the basement were expected to survive. The boy's father, who was somewhere on the first floor and out of the line of fire, had not been injured.

It's taken me a long time to try to set down my feelings about this incident. At the time, it felt as if somebody had punched me in the stomach, and in ways it has taken me until now to get my breath back. I'm ashamed to say that it wasn't the boy's death that so disturbed me, but the fact that it happened in a place where my family and I had once been safe.

I recently spent most of a month building a Christmas surprise for my wife, a one inch to one foot scale replica of her ancestral home in the Nebraska sandhills. The original, no longer owned by her family, was a sprawling fourteen-room, two-story frame house built in 1884. Her great-grandparents and grandparents lived there. Her great-aunt, still living and 108 years old at the time I am writing this, was born there. Her father and his brothers and sister chased through those rooms as small children, and as girls my wife and her younger sister spent summers there, taking care of their invalid grandmother.

Day after day as I worked on this dollhouse, pasting up wall-paper, gluing in baseboards and flooring, I would feel my imagination fitting itself into the little rooms. At times I lost all sense of scale and began to feel grit from the sandhills under my feet on the kitchen linoleum, to smell the summer sun on the porch roof shingles. I had never lived in that house but I lived there during those moments, and as I worked, the shadows of wind-tossed trees played over the dusty glass of the windows. Now and then I would hear footsteps on the porch, approaching the door.

Immediately upon seeing the dollhouse on Christmas Eve, my wife began to recall the way it had been furnished when she was a girl, to talk about this piece of furniture being here and that one there. I watched her feed the goldfish in the dirty aquarium and sit down on the stiff, cold leather of the Mission sofa. I saw her stroke-damaged grandmother propped in her painted iron bed under the eaves. Listening to my wife, watching her open the tiny doors and peer into the tiny closets, I began to think about the way in which the rooms we inhabit, if only for a time, become unchanging places within us, complete in detail.

I clipped the article about the shooting and must have read it a hundred times those first few days. In a front-on photo-graph, like a mug shot, there stood the house, sealed off by yel-low police tape, looking baffled, cold, and vacant. Next to the picture was a row of slack-faced mug shots of the five arrested. They looked as empty as the house.

I mailed a copy of the article to my first wife. I wanted her to share the shock that I was suffering, like a distant explosion whose concussion had taken years to reach across a galaxy of intervening happenstance. At the site of where only the most common, most ordinary unhappiness had come to us—misunderstandings, miscommunications, a broken marriage like thousands and thousands of others—there had been a murder, three people had been wounded, and five were on their way through the courts and into prison, all for the want of a pound of cocaine that the article reported had never been there.

For several years in the early 1960s we'd rented the first floor, which included the use of the cellar, which I used as a study. We'd been married for three years and were then in our early twenties. Diana was a schoolteacher in a nearby town, and I worked as a clerk at an insurance company. While we lived there, Diana became pregnant, our son was born, and when we brought him home from the hospital we carried him in through that same side door where the murder took place.

I remember matted orange shag carpet inside the door and continuing down the steps to the cellar, and more of the same carpet on the damp concrete floor and glued to the walls. (I can't think of it now without seeing bloodstains.) At the foot of the stairs, in a mildewed, overstuffed chair I'd bought at a thrift shop, I studied for night classes at the university. In that room I painted a few amateur pictures by bad basement light, one of a towering grain elevator that I thought was pretty good but which I mislaid long ago. A life-sized nude of Diana disappeared while we were packing to leave that house for another across town. I wonder if someone doesn't have it nailed up over their basement bar. Perhaps over cocktails on football Saturdays their guests try to guess who that pretty young woman might have been.

Two quiet Latvian women rented the upstairs apartment. They had emigrated from Europe during the Second World War and spent spring, summer, and autumn on their knees beside beds of annual flowers they'd put in along the driveway. Olga was the older, then I suppose in her sixties. She had a badly curved spine, a shy smile, and from a forest near Dresden had seen wave after wave of Allied bombers. She told me that a thousand feet over the city the atmosphere stood in red columns of flame. Alida was handsome, dark-eyed, dark-haired, younger than Olga. Of the two, she was the less approving of the young couple who lived downstairs, who drank too much, who had a very barky dog.

When I think of the exterior of that house, their flowers are always in bloom—petunias, asters, pansies, bachelor's buttons, phlox—but when I remember Diana and me living there, it is always winter and we are closed in by heavy snow. The side door where the boy was killed opened onto the driveway, and the first thing I did on those blizzardy winter mornings was to open it to let out our black schipperke, Hagen, and watch him wade through the snow to pee and then turn back, a miserable look on his sharp little face. It was a cheap aluminum storm door with loose glass panes, icy to the touch. As I waited there I could hear the kitchen radio behind me, turned up loud so that Diana, who dreaded the twenty-mile drive when the roads were bad, could catch the list of schools that were to be closed for the day.

In a few weeks' time I could build a miniature version of that house, using the approximate measurements of memory, and as I worked with plywood and paper and glue I would be able to gradually remember almost everything about it. But I won't need to do that; since the murder I have often peered into those little rooms where things went good for us at times and bad at times. I have looked into the miniature house and seen us there as a young couple, coming and going, carrying groceries in and out, hats on, hats off, happy and sad.

As I stared at the newspaper article, every piece of our furniture took its place in the rooms. I could have reached in through the door of that photograph and with the tip of a finger rolled our antique dental chair over the floor. A friend's big painting of the Rolling Stones hung on the opposite wall. On the living-room floor was the plush white carpet I'd bought with money from a literary prize. It was always dirty. Down the hall and through a door to the left, our bed, rumpled and unmade, stood right where it stood when we were young parents, with Jeffrey's crib nearby, and by leaning forward a little I could hear the soft, reassuring sound of his breath.

It has been more than thirty years since we lived at 2820 R Street, Lincoln, Nebraska. I write out the full address as if to fasten it down with stakes and ropes against the violence of time. I hadn't thought about it often, maybe a few times a year. But it was our house again the minute I opened the paper that morning and saw its picture and the faces of the people who had struck it with terrible violence. They didn't look sorry; they looked as if they'd do it again if they could.

Now and then since the murder I find myself turning into that decaying neighborhood and down that street, slowing to look at our house. The window shades are drawn on what were once such bright, welcoming rooms. Nobody lives there now, as far as I can tell. On snowy days there are no tracks up the drive to that flimsy side door.

I lean down, I try to fit myself inside. Even after thirty years there still might be the smell of Olga and Alida's salt herring being cooked upstairs, and on the first floor the fragrance of phlox, a few stalks in a water glass. For thirty years I had put it all firmly behind me, but like a perfect miniature it had waited in a corner of my heart, its rooms packed with memories. The murder brought it forward and made me hold it under the light again. Of course I hadn't really forgotten, nor could I ever forget how it feels to be a young father, frightened by an enormous and threatening world, wondering what might become of him, what might become of his wife and son.

Only a year after Diana, Jeff, and I moved away and into another house across town, the marriage came apart, and I began to learn to be a single father. From time to time Jeff came to visit me at the home of friends who had taken me in. The dead boy, too, had gone to visit his father.

If my luck in this life had been worse I might have been that other father, occupied by some mundane task, perhaps fixing a leaky faucet, when my son went to answer the door. But I was lucky, and my son was lucky, and today, long after the murder, finding myself imagining that damp cellar room, peering down into it as if looking into a miniature cellar, I don't hear shots or see blood on the steps. I hear only soft sounds: my breath as I sit with my book, Diana's stockinged feet as she pads along the hall above me, and water running into the bathtub as she gets ready to give our baby a bath.

The landlord, who owned a little doughnut shop, died many years ago. He had once lived in that house. His wife had Alzheimer's disease and sometimes arrived bewildered at our door, wanting us to let her in. She too is gone. If I were building a miniature of that house I would stand her at the door, clenching her purse in both hands, her hat on crooked.

The flowers that grew along the driveway are thirty years past their season and their beds are only dust today. My friend who painted the Rolling Stones has died. Olga and Alida, having survived the horrors of war to come to the new world and take a little pleasure in simple flowers, they too are gone. I've noticed lately when I've driven past that the porch has begun to slope toward the street, as if to pour our ghosts out the front door and onto the buckled sidewalk. And I am not that young father anymore, but a man who is slowly becoming a baffled old woman who hammers and hammers at a door, wanting to be let in again, knowing by instinct that something good must still be waiting just inside.

2003

Right Hand

This old hand with which I am writing,
holding its pen and pecking its way
across the paper like a hen, has pulled me,
clucking with little discoveries,
across more than seventy years, a sometimes
muddy, sometimes frozen barnyard
where, looking back, it seems that every day
was rich with interest, both underfoot
and just an inch or two ahead of that.

About the Author

The publication of this book, Ted Kooser's thirteenth full-length collection of poems, coincides with his seventy-fifth birthday. In 2004 he was appointed U.S. Poet Laureate and served two terms. His 2004 collection of poems from Copper Canyon Press, *Delights & Shadows,* was awarded the Pulitzer Prize. Kooser is Presidential Professor of English at the University of Nebraska–Lincoln and lives on an acreage near Garland, Nebraska, with his wife, Kathleen Rutledge. He has a son, Jeff, and two granddaughters, Margaret and Penelope.

Poetry is vital to language and living. Since 1972, Copper Canyon Press has published extraordinary poetry from around the world to engage the imaginations and intellects of readers, writers, booksellers, librarians, teachers, students, and donors.

WE ARE GRATEFUL FOR THE MAJOR SUPPORT PROVIDED BY:

THE PAUL G. ALLEN
FAMILY FOUNDATION

Lannan

THE MAURER FAMILY
FOUNDATION

OFFICE OF ARTS & CULTURE
SEATTLE

Anonymous

John Branch

Diana and Jay Broze

Beroz Ferrell & The Point, LLC

Janet and Les Cox

Mimi Gardner Gates

Gull Industries, Inc.
on behalf of William and Ruth True

Linda Gerrard and Walter Parsons

Mark Hamilton and Suzie Rapp

Carolyn and Robert Hedin

Steven Myron Holl

Lakeside Industries, Inc.
on behalf of Jeanne Marie Lee

Maureen Lee and Mark Busto

Brice Marden

Ellie Mathews and Carl Youngmann as
The North Press

H. Stewart Parker

Penny and Jerry Peabody

John Phillips and Anne O'Donnell

Joseph C. Roberts

Cynthia Lovelace Sears and Frank Buxton

The Seattle Foundation

Dan Waggoner

Charles and Barbara Wright

The dedicated interns and faithful
volunteers of Copper Canyon Press

The Chinese character for poetry is made up of two parts: "word" and "temple." It also serves as pressmark for Copper Canyon Press.

~~~

The interior is set in Miller, a "Scotch Roman" designed by Matthew Carter in 1997. The book title is set in Linotype Centennial, designed by Adrian Frutiger for the 1986 centennial of the Linotype machine. Book design by VJB/Scribe. Printed on archival-quality paper.